SOME COMMENTS ON EARLIER BOOKS BY DANIEL J. LANGTON

"These poems have a lovely pacing and interior radiance."
Tess Gallagher

*". . . superbly written, beautifully controlled, and yet
continually freshened by a kind and fresh imagination."*
Robert Bly

*". . . such a beauty, so moving, so beautifully made that
I have to tell you that it is one of the
finest lyrics in the language."*
William Carlos Williams

*"These poems have a lovely, understated
directness and restraint."*
Amy Glynn Greacen

"Daniel J. Langton's poems are a pleasure to read."
Paul Muldoon, poetry editor The New Yorker

*"The poems I have known before are as fresh as ever.
The new ones shimmer."*
Pamela Skewes-Cox

*"Only an Andrew Wyeth snowscape possesses the mental
loneliness and beauty captured in these poems."*
James Finn Cotter

"And he's a good kisser."
Eve Langton, who should know

DURING OUR WALKS

BY
DANIEL J. LANGTON

BLUE LIGHT PRESS ❖ 1ST WORLD PUBLISHING

1ˢᵗ WORLD
PUBLISHING

SAN FRANCISCO ❖ FAIRFIELD ❖ DELHI

DURING OUR WALKS
Copyright ©2011 by Daniel J. Langton

1ST WORLD LIBRARY
809 S. 2nd Street
Fairfield, Iowa 52556
www.1stworldpublishing.com

BLUE LIGHT PRESS
1563 45th Avenue
San Francisco, California, 94122
www.BlueLightPress.com

BOOK & COVER DESIGN
Melanie Gendron
www.melaniegendron.com

COVER ART
"Avenue of Luxembourg Gardens"
Vincent Van Gogh, 1884

AUTHOR
Dan Langton
P.O. Box 170012
San Francisco, California, 94117
www.DanLangton.com

AUTHOR PHOTOGRAPH
E.E. Van Brunt

FIRST EDITION

LCCN 2011931076

ISBN 978-1-4218-8609-1

FOR MARK

ACKNOWLEDGMENTS

Some of these have appeared in *Witness* and *Over the Transom*, and I am grateful to their editors.

This book is a series of monologues
by the village explainer to a recent arrival.

DURING OUR WALKS

I

Mind if I walk with you? I've always had a companion on my walks, but they fall away. My pace ain't much, I see you didn't have any trouble catching up with me.

We can stop here for a while if you want, get to know each other rather better than in those crowds at Tolliver's Fish and Brew. Ordinarily you can see the lake, but not with this fog.

I've been thinking about Sunday School. And, you know, that big battle with Satan. I mean, a real war it was, they say, and then you telling Marie last night that there can't be a God with so much evil in the world.

And then I said to myself, if there was a war, then there had to be a peace treaty. There's always a treaty.

Now you can see the lake. Ain't it pretty? O' course, anywhere it rains its pretty.

So I see a treaty. With sub-clauses and stuff, but with one big article: God and Satan would pick a tiny, out-of-the-way planet, like you said we are. And God would create the plants and Satan the animals.

Problems would come up, sure. Like Satan would want cats, and God would answer: only if there are dogs. And bees, there'd be a hubbub about bees, since flowers need them. And the crazy things. Like animal-eating plants. And vegetarians.

And down in the sea, where you can't see. Dolphins, sure, but Satan made the octopus in his own image, if you ask me. And, and this was just like the devil, he made us to look like God.

Sure explains a lot.

1

II

And then Donna got thick and started to forget names and so she called everybody Honey. Charles didn't mind that, he liked that, so we all went along. I mean, they had been married half a hundred years and they still stepped in puddles because they were looking at each other.

And then she didn't come out any more and then she died. People said to themselves; their children are dead, he mustn't stand at the grave alone, I'll be there. Only everybody thought the same thing, and it was the biggest funeral we ever had.

Charles stayed home after that and whittled ships, fished on gentle days. Except, that first Christmas Eve after, he came to Tolliver's Fish and Brew and got drunk. And told us.

After she didn't know who she was, they would go to bed and he would say, you are Sapphire, a slave girl. Which surprised me, them being colored and all. Or: You are the only woman in the white fleet. Or, my favorite: You are Sheba. He would give her flowers, weeds if there were none, and say they were offerings from, what did he call it, The Admiring Throng.

One day Charles fell out of his boat and no one was around and it took some time to find him. He had two trout.

III

There was the time Tommy fell in the well. Not that boys weren't always falling into wells; there was a joke that some fellas had hoisted more boys than fish in their time. No, Tommy was different, Tommy decided he didn't want to come up.

Have you ever tried to talk a boy out of something by talking down a well? It makes you feel as silly as talking to fish, though I'll grant I've done that, and with the same result.

There's some as put little stands into the wall of their well, so you can stand up down there if the water is high and sit if it is low. Tommy just sat there, saying no thank you, sir to each of us as we talked. We could see him real good, but nobody made a move to go down there and argue. He had a good reppatation, not crazy or mean, played baseball good for someone as was small for his age. It was a puzzle, and it got to be more of a puzzle as it got darker. He was so stubborn and so cheerful people went to their dinner. Him being an orpan and all, there was no parents there, and the guy from County never come.

Who knows when it was that everybody was gone? And Tommy sitting in the dark? What we know is he took one of the ropes we threw in and grounded and let himself out and walked to the Parker house whose well it was and took some clothes from a hamper and left his own and never went back to County or nowhere else. Which is how my Josh became left fielder.

IV

Well, then, there was Joey, around then when his daddy died.
Joey had this condition, couldn't close his mouth, though he sure
tried, and he walked like he'd been shot but didn't want to let on.
His mom worked at Pause Tolliver's Dry Goods Establishment.
Why his parents called him Pause is a good story too. Anyway,
Joey's mom with the unpronounceable last name so's she was
always called Joey's Mom was the best cook in the state, even
other cooks said so; even mean other cooks said so. Of course,
other kids made fun of Joey, there were some rock-throwing
incidents, even though she was a widow and all, her husband
died of what Doctor Tolliver called obesity, which sounds just
awful. But the adults handled the rock-throwing, and then they
seen what had happened, and they started throwing rocks at
him theirselves. Well, pebbles, really, and kind of gently thrown.
And Joey would go home and tell his mom, he could talk, sort
of, and she would come and sit with the ones responsible, and
they would be sorry and get next to tearful and she would snap
her purse shut and say, Well, that's all right then and we should
settle this over a nice dinner. And the pebble throwers would
go over there and have a nice dinner, and never even so much
as bring a pie. She never noticed they always flung the pebbles
on a day there would be a full moon, so they could find their way
home. Becky Tolliver, that's Anaton Tolliver's wife, said Mrs.
Joey's mom was on to it, but couldn't figure out any other way to
get people to dinner. And o'course that's how she met Isaac, who
was always peppering Joey, and who gave her a pronounceable
name and was a happy man until the day he died.

V

Every dog in the world has been born since good o'l Bobby died.
They can't have known him, but they seem like they all took
after him.

You said last night at Tolliver's Fish and Brew as how that
Frenchman said animals can't think, which only proves he never
had a dog. Either that, or French dogs is a race apart.

Now, Bobby. The deeper I went into his world, the deeper I saw
it was. I learnt and learnt. I listened to his eyes.

He would have forgiven anything. Not twice, mind. He didn't
know there's places where people eat dog. Well, hell, there's
places where people eat people.

Maybe there's another planet. Another try. Where you don't
have to eat, you are movable plants, where dogs don't have to be
wary. Where people don't say things as silly as Trump Tolliver
said. "Precious stones." My, my.

Of course, there'd still be dying. There will allus be dying.
That's what makes Life what it is.

VI

Watch out for that.

There's three kinds of city women. Born there, country girls as go there, them as goes from city to city.

There's reasons to go from the country, you can see that in them that don't go. Take Bessie. Our waitress? Whose real name is Ava, but call me Bessie? When she divorced Clinton on account of the drinking, she said there was eleven eligible men around, and nine of them was shorter than she was. So she stayed on, and became the slap-the-ass waitress, you know, the one who laughs too easily.

Or Judith Tolliver. You'll never meet her. She never married, and never come back. They say you learn that in college, that they wait for you in college. It's hard to say.

Or Jeremy and Clinton. One lived with his mother and one alone, until their fifties, until people would put up with Clinton moving into Jeremy's Mother's house. Why? Might as well ask a cow.

There's a lot of crackle. We get snowed-in more ways than one. I remember Julia's face when she was told Ronald Reagan used to be married to that lady on her favorite television show. No meanness, no meanness, just no understanding. It's like someone was to say they've decided to live in Antarctica.

City women. I'm glad you told me about that, about with your wife. You won't find sympathy here. Just blank, pleasant faces. There's a reason people a long time ago decided to be dressed all the time, no matter what.

VII

My Jill told me last night she'd signed us up for cremation.
Seems there was a sale.

I thought of it this morning, putting on my socks. I tried to
imagine my toes burst into flames. O' course, I wouldn't get to
see it, would I?

A small, straight-laced place like this, come up with so many
ways to go. Chub, you never met him, announcing at the Fort'a
July picnic that his corpse, his word, his corpse would go to the
county hospital for students to study and to take final exams on.
I went to high school with him, for Pete's sake.

And Una Proxmire, gone too, who left a will, something you
hardly ever see if you're not a Tolliver. Left all her money to
the high school. They bought an English dictionary which is
books and books. Jim, you remember him, the one that don't
drink, he said no student ever has taken a look in it. Anyway,
Una also left a note with the will that she wanted to be buried in
the clothes she happened to die in. Sarah Proxmire said at the
service that since nobody had ever seen her naked, now was no
time to start. I thought that was just snippy.

And there's Tom. I love that man. His two sons are in France.
Not in the same graveyard, but in France. Tom went there
once, shouldn't have gone alone, but he only got to go because
of Sadie's insurance. Got in a fight with a Frenchie about what
Tom will just keep calling a lack of respect. I guess they couldn't
afford to bring all those dead boys back home after World War II.

And then there's the people who talk about heaven. Like Walter
says he is going to ask God to make the Bing cherry season
longer. And those that want God to interfere with sports.

Even Tom. He says everyone gets to be their favorite age. So he'll be thirty six. But he worries, because Sadie once said she was happiest when she was twelve.

Cremation. I thought they only did that in crowded places, like India or England. My Jill says we can have our ashes mingled, even if it's years apart. I don't know, I guess God can do anything. He'll find us.

VIII

Well, it seems yesterday was a Holy Day of Obligation. But every day can't be that. Except it can. If their private life's like mine. Yesterday was the anniversary of Chance's death. You met his Esther. Chance drove way too fast. He called himself the ugly Paul Newman. I'll tell you, the telephone pole didn't know he was a good guy with eleven grandchildren who will only get to guess at what he was like.

And birthdays. I used to joke women have one every three years. I'm not joking no more. If Jill ain't wrapping she's mailing.

Sometimes I get to thinking. Look, when I was a kid we had a big Holy Day of Obligation. The Feast of the Circumcision. I ain't joshin'. I can see how they would give that up. Young girls saying: What's a circumcision? Or better: Show me. Or they didn't want people reflecting on what they do to a man's thing. Or his being Jewish. Or thinking about him too much anyroad. Like how come he never got married. And only hung around with guys. And seemed to be maybe prolly too close to his mother. Or did the popes just make Him sound like Italian men.

I hope I haven't offended you. Everybody noticed and notices you never been in either church. Yet you don't go anywhere the local sinners gather. People say you're writing a novel about us; I tell them city people sleep late.

If it is a novel, you can leave out who told you what.

IX

Crisp, ain't it? Days like this feel like a message.

I read that book you gave me. That's a lie, I read in it. And you didn't give it, you lent it. And you don't often see a book where even the pictures make you squint your brain.

Science is all so strange. I see what he means, but I sure can understand people it upsets. It must of been nice being sure of what people used to be sure of.

I remember. It all started four thousand years ago. We were the center of the universe. Stars so's we could sail at night. In the image of Him.

Four thousand years ago? Four billions? Who cares? I mean, I don't care when it started; what I do care about is, Why Then? Maybe there was three hundred and sixty trillion years of nuttin' and then God got tired of looking at his angels and said, "I just made up a game that needs people." That once. That time. Why Then?

And then last night I got to thinking: We're off in a corner of the universe. The center, where Heaven is, the book says is billions of light years from here. But the book also says that nuttin' can travel faster than the speed of light. So everybody who ever died and went to Heaven is still on their way there. And will be for quite a while. Maybe that's what that dark matter is.

Religions seem to get the big stuff right and the little stuff's silly. All those priests and monks and rabbis thinking up stuff to pass the time, after seeing to it they had a lot of time. It worries me.

X

Yeah, I know. Well, I didn't know you were divorced. I figured,
well, we all did, you were old enough to have a wife so you had
lost her, died tragically, run off, no, no one was about to ask.
But you divorced her? And you left a daughter with her?

There aren't any divorced people here, except for Bernice and
Clinton and his ex. Oh, you know as well as I do, there are
people living separate, like the Jewish couple that has two
entirely different houses. Mike goes over there one night a
week, every week, for dinner. People say it's their holy day, but
why would that matter?

And, you know, everybody knows about you and little Junie
at Tolliver's Fish and Brew. Like you sit there in the morning
at the counter instead of at one of Bessie's tables and look at
Junie till your coffee's cold. It would be a snark if she were the
town beauty, but no one can see what you see. I mean, her last
ninety-six dates was with truck drivers.

Love. I wonder if it's in the dictionary. Take a genius to define
it. Songs stumble all over theirselves. Comedians can't stop. To
a tennis player love means nothing. I like that one. I love ice
cream. I have a love seat. Lordy.

I know what it is for me, but nobody else. After I married Jill I
realized that, for good reason, she was going to go to Hell. And
that I would have to commit some mortal sin, and keep it up, so
that I'd be sure to go to Hell.

Anyway, if I understand it right, love is the medicine and sex is
the side effect.

XI

Look, I can ask you, you're a big city boy and I'm always anxious
to learn. When did the word become "gay"? When I was a kid it
was AC/DC, which worked perfect for me because I understood
electricity about as much as I understood a yearning for the
digestive track.

Jill says it's all in the Bible, but she would use the Bible for a
doorstop. I allus felt sorry for them because they have to give
up on having kids and life is a desert without kids. Oh, I know
there are guys who seem to have it both ways, but they really
don't. I mean, you never hear of a guy sneaking off from his boy
friend to go see his girl friend.

I think in the city, all crowded together, you have to be tolerable.
Here, we just let it slip and slide, like it ain't happening. Like
the two truckers who allus seem to get here at the same time,
order chicken-fried steak, and sit off by theirselves. What's it to
me? most people say. But I notice they notice. Or Jeremy and
Clinton, as far as I know.

Folks, I notice, know love when they see it. Years ago we had a feller, dead now, no need for names, he had a neighbor who shot this feller's dog for no damned reason. The feller shot him. The jury was out fifteen minutes. A week or so later one of the jury brought him a pup out at his place.

I can't stand on a perch and crow because God made me normal. And I know the majority allus passes laws saying that what they ain't doing theirselves must be a crime.

And actors that play gay men. Do they have to be gay? I mean, the guys in Rotary, one night a year, all got up in grass skirts, lipstick, circles of rouge, what are they doing? What are they feeling?

And that gets me back to God. What was He thinking, not making all that impossible. The meanest man ever lived wouldn't toy with you like that.

XII

Let's go have breakfast. Jill didn't feel like none, and won't make it for one.

There are people who said you came here to die. What are you, forty? And then, you're such a finicky eater. Coffee and a doughnut, and you fool with the coffee. And in the evenings two beers, and you never finish the second.

So they figured you allus lived in the big city and a Doctor says, the pollution has clamped your lungs, and you thought, Not Here. Why else would a guy take a room at Esther's, hell, the only room she's got, and read books he brought with him; reads them all day, she says?

It was funny how that made people take to you. I mean, you have no family within a hundred miles, you talk like a teacher just let out of solitary confinement, you didn't volunteer for the fire brigade, you seem to be no kind of an athlete, never even once tried to dance, just nursed that beer.

Of course, this is an older town. A lot of people been diagnosed.
Doctor Tolliver loves his jokes; he says I will "die o' beetes."

I wonder if everybody is sure that everybody's gonna die. I
mean, you're immortal til you do. Some still think you came
here to die, though Johnny Vourteen thinks you're in the
Witness Protection Program. People know I know you, they ask
if you're dying and I answer, Who ain't?

That story you told about gorillas. Like everybody in the old
days thought about what they would be like all the time and
then they found them and then they stopped thinking about
them. I thought about sickness in my blood. Now I don't think
about it at all. I mean, no matter how anxious you are to get the
mail, you calm down when it comes. Jill said, if God can take
Cary Grant, then He's liable to take anybody.

XIII

Jill ain't constant. Everybody knows it, but I can't talk about it with anyone because nobody knows it. I can talk to you about it, because you won't have kids here and grand-kids here who would talk about it. There was an original Amos Tolliver who shot himself in the head. A hundred years ago. People talk about it.

It started finally after our boy was born. She had Doctor Tolliver fix her. Didn't ask me, but she did tell me. She healed up, was moody for a while, and then it started.

My dad drank too much. Often. My mom said even a good man can have a weakness, and I would help her lift him into bed. Well, Jill is a good person, doesn't hurt anybody, knows what's off limits. Never in our house.

We've never talked about it. Can you believe that? It's true. I pretend I'm asleep when she gets home. I wish I could lose my sense of smell.

It was hard on the kids. I know they all left as soon as they could. They love her, but I know they think I'm wrong for not chaining her up or something. Yes, they love her, but there never was a time in their lives when she wasn't mom. I can remember a time I never knew her, and then I did, and life went to Technicolor, like the Wizard of Oz. I could never go back to black and white, no matter what the story is.

We won't talk about this again.

XIV

Every girl I ever made love with is dead. I don't include Jill, I mean made love without a license.

There's a reason. They were much older than I was, though lively, they were wild hares. I don't see them in my head, not their faces, I see a floating black patch with two nipples floating about it, God forgive me.

I think of all the wildness, the can't-eats, the clamminess, the throwings-up, the heart beating in your ears. And now they're still, as still as still gets. What was I doing? What were they doing? I could have done it in a cow's nose, like Brent and Lee did. I could have turned it off, as they say nuns and priests do.

I'll bet some do.

No names, but there was one, standing in the lake to her waist and taking her top off with the sun on her, was anyone ever so alive? We know we're gonna die, is that why some do it, is that why some don't do it?

Shadows now, though I can hear their voices plain. I tell myself they're a secret, but everyone in town knows the four funerals in my life I didn't go to.

XV

Yeah, well, there are still people in town who wonder why you came, wonder why you're here. I mean, you don't even fish. For God's sake, everybody fishes. Even has rules, you eat everything you catch or you give it to someone to eat who has got too old to fish.

They all find you likeable, though Farley says to me one night, Jim, do you look up those words he uses to see if he's funnin' us? I don't, but I did once. Laconic. You said that of Henry Fonda. I revere Henry Fonda. I was surprised to find out he was from Greece.

The big theory now is that you are writing a book about the Tollivers, though there are already two, which they brought out theirselves.

I guess if you're doing that, and I'm not asking, you have to do research, read other people's letters, though who writes letters nowadays. I guess you could write a pretty thorough life just by reading their credit card statements. You'd know where they were every day of the week, what they were buying, what they were eating, where they were staying.

Am I going to be in the book?

XVI

I do funny things when I'm trying to sleep. Long division.
Square roots. Things I was good at at school.

So last night I said to myself: What if I went to bed on the last
day of 1899 and woke up on January 1, 2000. What would I
have missed? Babe Ruth. Marilyn Monroe. FDR.

I mean, those were dreamy times. Sherlock Holmes and all.
The whole world at peace. Nobody had old-timer's disease. And
who would never have lived? Stalin. Hitler. That creepy guy in
China. There'd be no atom bomb and no atomic junk because of
it. And, excuse me, people would still know their place.

And women would be virtuous.

There was this guy on the radio, talked about what America
would be like if we hadn't gone into either of the World Wars.
Maybe we'd have what I'm talking about. Take over Canada and
Mexico and let the rest of the world go by. Maybe then baseball
would be like it used to be.

I guess medicine got better, but guns got to be so much better.
A guy doesn't know if the trigger is pulled by a saint or a nut, it
just goes off. They're just too easy to use.

No, we could have missed all that. Let the Chinese figure it out
for theirselves, just raise crops so the city people can eat while
selling things to each other. And paintings that look like people.
Thank God for cameras.

XVII

Someday I will be dead for thirty-two years.

I mean, everything will go along the same, as though you were here, it's just that every year I will have been dead longer.

What? Oh. Thinking of Pendleton. Only person from around here went to Europe and never came back. Pendleton, for God's sake. His name was John. John. His mother was a Pendleton.

He died the day Jimmy Carter was sworn in. Paper was full of it the next day, his picture right next to the new president. So this morning I realized it was thirty-two years.

I sure as hell think about death more than when I was twenty. You look at your eighth grade graduation picture and you tick off the names. Even my Josh and Janet have lost friends, God damned automobiles. Greeting cards say, I will love you forever. Ain't but one thing you're going to do forever.

I can't believe I won't remember the last thing I ever do. That all I knew just goes that-a-way. That someday, maybe thirty-two years later, there won't be anyone who remembers me.

XVIII

Dogs. I'm too old to have a dog. I do remember the only prayer
I ever heard I'd be willing to say. "Dear God, help me to become
the man my dog thinks I am."

Too old to have a dog, now ain't that a thing. I suppose I could
get a real old dog with arthritis, like Mary Bell has. But for me
it was running along with Bobby running along beside me. That
dog never did learn to walk, he was either curled up or running
like hell.

Dogs is for men who don't understand women, cats is for women
who are jealous about the thing between men and dogs. Yeah, I
know there are men who are part women and some women are
part men, which explains people who are a mix of dogs and cats.
But a true dog-man knows, he can tell, he knows his dog is his
contact with the rest of the animal world. I don't mean that's
good, it can be good or bad. But it's there. Watch a boy watching
a dog have pups. You can feel it, you can see it.

There's a town in Europe, it was on the news, that has never
allowed dogs. Go there, study the young men. I'll bet you'll
learn something you don't want to know.

You say the Muslims don't have dogs? That sure explains a lot.

XIX

You know, when you first got here I decided I had the time
to show you around the town and around the valley, get you
acquainted. I never thought I'd get interested in books you lent
me, or those that Ida at the library had to send for. I gather
none of them lived a life as would fill anybody with envy.

And then there's role models. Before you got here, a couple of
years ago, the middle school principal ran off with one of his
teachers. Both of them married. What are the children to make
of that? The kids at the time are older now, and they snicker
when they talk of the principal and his "homilies." And the only
minister who ever actually made his home in town was stumble-
drunk each morning as he came out to get the paper.

It always brings me back to Ben-Ellen. That's what everybody
calls them. They started dating at sixteen, and they're in their
eighties, and no one's ever seen one without the other. So you
have to say Ben-Ellen "he" and Ben-Ellen "she."

Ben-Ellen "he" told me how heaven is individually designed for
each family. Right now he is the happiest man as can be, so
he figured out he has died, has no memory of that, that he is in
heaven, and his life, in quotation marks, will just go on forever.
That way he doesn't have to dread the thump in the next room,
or calling up from the cellar and Ben-Ellen "she" doesn't answer,
and you got the long walk up to the house proper to look.

We all ponder. You are trying to work it out, and I take stabs
at it, and maybe we just have to figure it out for ourselves, each
and only.

XX

You ever watch the History Channel? You would think that history was another way to spell war. And all that Hitler stuff. You think sixty years ago people were all that fascinated by what happened sixty years before them? I don't think so.

I know fellas were in the second World War. I know fellas were in Korea. Vietnam. Iraq. And now that other place. And I'm not even counting the little bitty ones, because nobody from here was in those. Those guys are all what you said about yourself, dour. Were you in the military? I didn't think so. I guess you can get dour on your own. I was a little too young and then a little too old for the service.

War. Such a big country, with no one to fight. So we fought the Indians. We even fought the Mexicans. You don't see the Mexicans fighting those weak countries south of them. And those generals wearing rows and rows of ribbons, what was that you said, they look like fruit salad. For me, the only reason a general ever won a battle is that he was fighting another general; you may notice those countries that don't have generals, like Viet Nam, can beat anybody.

People will always put up money for a war, and money for monuments later, but they hate to put up money for those who got maimed, and the only doctors what join the Army are those suspicious of human beings.

I'm glad you never went. I'm more comfortable with those who never went. Those who did go always seem to have looked in a door and seen what no one should see. And they say, I don't want to talk about it, and all their eyes do is talk about it.

XXI

Drummond told me you talked to him about getting the Odeon
opened again. My God, you're useful. That drive-in over to
Squamish never worked somehow. Summers only, and in
Summer it seemed like you had to wait until nine for the picture
to start, and most people around here start yawning at nine.

But the Odeon. You went with your folks at first and got a
Peppermint Patty and sometimes you got more excited by the
coming attractions than by the big movie. Later you went with
them guys you liked, and you had your first cigarette there.
Then you went with a girl, with everybody craning to see who it
was as you came to the ticket window. Then one day your wife,
then one day your wife and kids.

There were no foreign films then. No films about drugs. No girls
without blouses. The church social would end with everybody
with their fill of chicken salad going in a group to a movie, with
Cary Grant or Gary Cooper. Sure, you sometimes wanted the
bad guy to get away, but you felt funny when he did.

It was what people talked about, that and Li'l Abner and
Dick Tracy. Cause everybody saw the same movie, even if
on different nights. Nowadays people are in their homes and
they're watching fifteen different channels from each other, and
when they have coffee together they have to talk politics.

People say they want their country back. What they mean is
what they want is their young days back, time will come when
our kids will be longing for now. But to me, it was walking to
the movie, the movie, and walking home from the movie. The
three best things.

XXII

That there was the most hilarious night of my life. I got a reppatation as a story teller, but I come in second now, you can tell a story. Dry as toast.

Of course everybody got into it, but half didn't believe you for a minute. Why would someone like you see a psychiatrist? Sure, you have had grief, everybody has, but grief is to be dealt with. I guess I believe you, but then again maybe you're a writer trying things on.

That bit about the famous feller who went to one for fifteen years, and the story about a shrink for dogs. If a dog went for fifteen years he would have gone for his whole life. I wouldn't send my dog, any dog, to a shrink, but I might go to a dog who was a psychiatrist. He would just look at you until you figured out for yourself what you were thinking.

And what Henry said: that when people who live in places like this figure out they're weird they move to the city, so that's where the shrinks are, like that fella who robbed banks. I don't know, I never had much use for people who hear a different drummer, but I sure would have liked to know that drummer.

I think we're all afraid of being exactly alike. I think we're all kind of sneakily pulling for the guy who's getting messages from Mars on his toothbrush radio.

Maybe shrinks are adapting people to what's been done to the world. Maybe sane people are just those who have learned to control their nuttiness in public. If anyone knew my ten goofiest thoughts I'd be locked up for sure, or at least have to talk to one of those guys who won't look at you.

XXIII

You never met Paul, he died a few months before you moved here. We used to walk together, him and me, even in the hills. I wish he were here, I would've liked to walk, the three of us.

I can tell you what he was like from a couple of stories. People pretend you can do that with almost anyone, like at funerals, but those are pass-the-time stories. But Paul. You could do that.

We went walking right after Doc Tolliver told Paul about the cancer. I asked him if he had one thing, one thing, the power to leave one thing behind, what would it be? And he said, right off, I'd fix it so nobody would know how old they are.

And then he was in that hospice place and sent word he didn't want visitors. I got a letter from him. It said, Make sure your children know how to dance.

Paul didn't grow up here. His daddy, the professor, had him late in life and his mother died having him, and he grew up in a college town until his dad retired and came here to study plants. Paul always said he had to get out of here and then to everyone's astonishment, he bought Jesse's farm. His dad left him money, and the farm slowly lost it.

People noticed two things about Paul. He didn't have a TV and he didn't invite anybody over. He stayed a bachelor, there are plenty of bachelors around here, the girls leave for greener pastures and it takes money to get married. But all his friends were married men, and he was polite to their wives, but antsy around them, especially Jill.

There are those who are special, there never was one like them, never will be again. Nature must be confidence itself, thinking she can keep doing that.

26

XXIV

It's just down there, toward the edge of the canyon. It's got a red
roof. It's damned little, a shack, mostly. Yeah, now you've got it.

Billy said he only meant to shove her, but nobody was having
any of that. Niles Tolliver, everyone called him the persecuting
attorney, was as happy as a boy with a new dog. It was the only
murder around here for generations, everyone said, but I think
there have been one or two clever poisoners, especially in the
First Family.

Oh, I'm against murder. Everybody hears nowadays about serial
killers, but when Billy killed Lorene he killed the babies she
never had, and the babies those babies never had, to the end of
the world. But they never should have put him to death. People
say, an eye for an eye, but I notice everyone who says that has
two of 'em.

There was a feller on the news, a drug dealer, who sent someone
to kill a guy. President Bush was asked to stop the execution of
the drug dealer but he said No, sending someone to kill someone
was too fiendish and terrible. So he sent someone over to kill
him.

I watched a TV show where they fatally injected a prisoner. A
guy in a white outfit stuck a needle in the guy's arm. But before
he did, he wiped the spot with alcohol. Why? I'll tell you why.
He wanted out of there, he wanted to be in the world of real
people. He knew the killing was wrong, the alcohol was him
asking for forgiveness.

He won't get mine. Well, not for a long time.

XXV

No.   No.   No.   I'll just sit on this rock.   No.   William?

William. Who would have thought it? Who would think it of
anyone? He was Jill's classmate, for God's sake. Lived the same
life we did, saw the same things. I was having lunch with him
when somebody came in and said the president was shot. He
was putting ketchup on his fries. Didn't even stop.

I think God invented dreams so we would go to sleep. They don't
mean anything, they're just to keep us from perpetual dark.
Who would go to sleep if it were all dark, all black, all the time,
until you woke up and could see the mantle? Sweet dreams,
people say, encouraging you to sleep.

I suppose there is power in knowing. I, William Richards, will
die on such-and-such a date, even though I am in good health
and alert. I won't even wait for the Social Security check,
which would have helped Martha bury me. I will write a note,
something everyone will read and ponder over. I will be talked
about for many, many funerals on.

I appreciate your telling me you thought about it. If there had been a gun in the hotel room, that sort of thing, like you said. I've never given it a serious thought, myself. It's like you said about the universe, everywhere else nothing is happening, or, at the most, bugs, though some scientists believe otherwise. You got to try, you got to try. Have you seen Martha? The two worst things you can do to another person, and he had done them both. And I admired him, I admired him, up to now. What does that say about me?

Death blinds you, the eternal dark. It also changes the way you think about people who have died. If ever somebody does come back from the dead, we'd change our opinion of them yet again.

We all think of Jesus on the cross and Jesus back again, saying Hello to everybody. Nobody talks about Jesus in that tomb. Three days. Three nights. That's a long time. Did he dream?

XXVI

I know, it's been a while. I haven't had the heart to go on walks.
Then to find out William left me his fishing gear. And the boat.
Though I don't think the boat is safe.

This is my first function since. I didn't think about it, about
them inviting you, but I'm glad they did. I guess you're getting
to be part of things.

Weddings. I guess you always remember your own. I remember
William saying, The bad thing is if you remember your parents'
wedding. I remember the night he said it. You could tell a lot by
the fellas who laughed and the fellas who didn't get it.

I wish them luck. I really do. Though nowadays they seem
to take it lightly, the young people. When I was going to the
movies a lot the hero was never divorced, and if a lady was
divorced, well, Watch Out, she was a home-wrecker. Now
it's like everybody is fooling around before marriage, during
marriage, gonna fool around when the marriage is over. And
doing the deed? That's like having a sandwich together.

I do believe marriage is forever. What is it going to be like
in heaven, with your two wives who have had three other
husbands? God will have some sorting to do.

They say it's a sacrament because Jesus went to a wedding. Well,
he went to the bathroom every day, so the smallest room in the
house should be a shrine? Excuse me, I guess that's going too far.

But take Adam. God gave him this naked Eve and said to them,
implied, Go to it. So answer me this. When he introduced them,
why didn't he marry them? On the spot. Adam could have had
Jesus as his Best man. Tell me that.

XXVII

I want to start off by thanking you. WE ARE NOT ALONE.
That was prolly the best TV show I ever saw. Not while we were
watching it, all those remarks and beer orderings, but later.
I lay awake until Jill got home just thinking about it. I told
Jill and she said, I didn't know that dump got that channel. I
figured from that she didn't want to talk about it.

All those fellows, and that woman doctor, talking about being
alone. And they were never alone, they were always with each
other, I smiled at that. But when they got all excited when they
thought they saw a dead bug or something in a Mars rock, that
got me quiet.

And they talk about time as though they knew time. And how
people will build time machines a thousand years from now and
come back here. And if those future people can, and if they will,
and if they did, then where are they? If they'd been here, it
would have been in the papers.

My theory is that space critters are a millions of an inch tall,
and they come here all the time in iddy bitty ships we can't see.
Or they came once, a long time back, looked around, and went
back home, saying, Scratch that one, Leave it alone, Nothing but
dinosaurs.

And yet I sympathize, wrong as they are I do. And I got a way to
help them. Tell them ferrets came from Pluto. Anteaters from
Saturn. Rabbits from Mercury. Dogs from happy old heaven.
They'll spend their lives studying them, never stop for a minute.

You wouldn't believe the relief they will feel at not being alone.

XXVIII

With all it has to do, I find it hard to credit that the sun has time
to burn me, ripen my pear.

Jill did show some interest in what you said. You know,
intelligent life on other planets. Like, does Jesus hop from
planet to planet, getting crucified? Not to mention Second
Comings. And Thirds, in really tough places. It sounds lively
but unlikely, like ants in snow. She says she can't find it fair
that the unknowable is vital.

I know you're curious about the Tollivers. They would make
anybody curious. Around here, among ourselves, they're called
the First Family. I allus figured the rest of us get along better
because they're there.

They made all their money starting a hundred years ago with
a brand of clothing. It was called Loungerie, bathrobes and
nightgowns and lay-around-in stuff. They said it was for regular
people, but I always thought it was for those who like their vice
versa.

I don't know why they never left the area. A few did, of course,
but not the main ones. Not one Tolliver has ever married a
Townie. Made babies with some, the ones with new cars, as they
say. But mostly they leave and come back with someone as is
used to money.

I'm glad they exist, like I'm glad of the English Royal Family. If
they weren't around to look at, there would be some as believe
you could breed humans and get better ones. One look at Prince
Charles on the TV would cure you of that one.

They seem to be thinning out. Diseases and quirks other people
don't seem to have. Even their horses and dogs shy too easy. I
feel for them, but I wouldn't miss them.

XXIX

I have always been fascinated by the truth. I mean, when you say, You're lovely, to a lady, or I love you, to a dog. Is the lady lovely, lovely to all? I'm sure you could find somebody who thought she was ugly. As for the dog, they don't know words, they know tone. There used to be dog acts in the Vaudeville, the guy would say sit up and the dog would lie down, always got a laugh. So you could say I hate you to a dog with the right tone and he would lick your hand, same as before.

There are people who say lying can be harmless, like How do you like my new hat? And there are those who say it is necessary, that it would be an awful world if we couldn't lie. I dunno, I do know it keeps me thinking.

I saw a TV show on the education channel. They left two monkeys alone with a banana, and they watched them. A monkey ate the banana. They stormed in and said to him—Who ate the banana? And he pointed at the other monkey. My God, monkeys can lie, and think nothing of it.

I remember a visiting preacher says every man knows what he is, and he's not talkin'. I remember I was at the parking lot of the school after a meeting. It was late. I came upon a woman. She nearly died of fright. I was hurt that anyone would be afraid of me. I wanted to say, well . . . I don't know what I wanted to say.

Have I lied? Very little. Can I be trusted to keep things to myself? Usually, but less and less as I get to know someone. And, after all, everyone I know I've known forever. Well, not you, but that will come.

I guess if I made up a world, if I populated it, it would be a town where nobody lied and everybody knew how to keep secrets. I think it would be warmer, more affectionate. Women in parking lots at night wouldn't be scared. Even if you said boo.

XXX

Politics. Yeah, I read the election results. Elections remind me that it's going to get colder soon.

First man I ever voted for was shot dead. I thought I shouldn't vote again. And then that Nixon. That he could rise to the top of politics told me a lot about politics.

What it is is admitting failure. You and I can't get along on a handshake, so we make rules and fellows to keep track of us and the rules. If there were no Ten Commandments wouldn't we all know what's in them? Years, years ago, I seen my eighteen year old Josh, sitting on the floor, a bug goes by, he raises his hand to smash it, and pulls back. What made him raise his hand? What made him pull it back? He didn't know no rules.

And then there's the rules we make up for to get the job. I remember until Reagan a divorced fellow couldn't get the job. And your family had to be from the north west of Europe. And you couldn't have an old run-in with the police, or smoked funny stuff, or gotten a girl in the family way, or if you had your doubts about God's mercy. That must leave the job to people who crochet. I remember someone saying, they usually only have daughters. As if that meant something. Maybe it does.

And then they get mad if you don't vote. Hold your nose and vote, they say. Of course, they mean vote for them. And then they judge the presidents. You ever notice, you can take the lists of presidents ever since we became a big powerful country, and you see who is considered great and you match them up with the number of boys killed in their just-starting lives and what do you see? Lincoln, Wilson, FDR, Johnson. The names and the numbers match. Maybe Bush Junior knew about that, wanted to make the list.

I'll bet people once lived life with the politics left out. There's people as how they got born, and lived, and married, and died, and the government didn't even know. I know, I'll bet it had its problems, not for everyone, but I would have liked to try it.

XXXI

Why Jill? I don't understand you. So little pleasure buying so
much pain. I mean, just one thing, she's old enough to be your
mother. Actual. I know her age, I know yours.

What happens, what goes through a person's mind? I have the
rest of my life to figure this out. I mean, with Jill it's been truck
drivers, what they call transients. Nobody ever sees anything
or says anything. They say, Jim's wife, Jim's to handle. I know
because it's what I'd say.

But you? Is that what cities are like? A million pebbles, but
you got to have the one next door. No wonder you got six locks
to a door. It must be the strangest feeling, that you got to have
something just because you can. We should make life as bright
as possible, not darken it.

Before you I walked with William, until he got so sad, before
that with Paul. I could have left them in a bed with Jill naked
and they would have got up and gone. And they are one-tenth as
smart as you are and never read philosophy or novels.

Maybe something will come of it. For the first time ever Jill is
sorry. Maybe you'll tell me that was your plan, remorse and
change, you're good at that, too good at that. But that's not it.
You'll give up the full thing for the fifteen minutes, is what you'll
do, and then tell yourself you did a good thing, if you just think
about it.

Here's your books back.

XXXII

I was driving around when this tune I love came on the radio. "Oh, they say you are leaving the valley." I know about it being about a woman, but I was only thinking about the first line.

I know people have theories of why I don't come around any more in the evenings, or even the now-and-then breakfast. I don't care. I must say, I was hoping you'd be the one stopped going.

So it's back to the city, and cocktail parties, and stories about the hicks. You're better than that, but you won't let yourself be better than that.

I finally figured out about Jill. You had to do something that couldn't be forgiven, you had to hit something so hard you would be sure it's dead. You had to do something that not only shouldn't be done, it couldn't be done. You liked it here and then you got bored, or you got everything out of it you could and you looked for the toilet paper.

I should pity you, but that would be like pitying a rock.

They'll talk about you for a spell. I won't go in evenings for a longer while. Then some day someone will look up from his paper at breakfast and say, Remember that feller stayed here for a while way back? Died in his sleep. So that's how he spelled his name.

And that will be that.

D aniel J. Langton was born in Paterson, New Jersey and raised in East Harlem with his brothers and sister. He is married to Eve and they have a son, Mark. They live in San Francisco, where he teaches English and Creative Writing at San Francisco State University. His poetry has appeared in such journals as the *Nation*, the *Paris Review*, the *Atlantic Monthly*, the *TLS*, the *Harvard Advocate* and the *Iowa Review*, and has been awarded the London Prize, the Devins Award, the Edgar Allan Poe Award and others. This is his seventh collection.

Daniel J. Langton was launched into a life of writing poetry by William Carlos Williams. As he tells the story, "When I was just starting out, I went to a reading by William Carlos Williams. Afterward I showed him a poem of mine, and he told me, *I don't care what you're doing, quit your job, and write nothing but poetry.* And that's what happened."

Printed in The United States of America

www.ingramcontent.com/pod-product-compliance
Lightning Source LLC
Chambersburg PA
CBHW032036090426
42741CB00006B/838